JOHN STOTT BIBLE STUDIES

12 Studies with Commentary for Individuals or Groups

Galatians

Experiencing the Grace of Christ

John STOTT

with Dale & Sandy Larsen

Inter-Varsity Press
Nottingham, England

IVP Connect
An imprint of InterVarsity Press
Downers Grove, Illinois

InterVarsity Press, USA
P.O. Box 1400, Downers Grove, IL 60515-1426, USA
World Wide Web: www.ivpress.com
Email: email@ivpress.com

Inter-Varsity Press, England
Norton Street, Nottingham NG7 3HR, England
Website: www.ivpbooks.com
Email: ivp@ivpbooks.com

InterVarsity Press®, USA, is the book-publishing division of InterVarsity Christian Fellowship/USA®, a student movement active on campus at hundreds of universities, colleges and schools of nursing in the United States of America, and a member movement of the International Fellowship of Evangelical Students. For information about local and regional activities, write Public Relations Dept., InterVarsity Christian Fellowship/USA, 6400 Schroeder Rd., P.O. Box 7895, Madison, WI 53707-7895, or visit the IVCF website at <www.intervarsity.org>.

Inter-Varsity Press, England, is closely linked with the Universities and Colleges Christian Fellowship, a student movement connecting Christian Unions in universities and colleges throughout Great Britain, and a member movement of the International Fellowship of Evangelical Students. Website: www.uccf.org.uk.

All Scripture quotations, unless otherwise indicated, are taken from the Holy Bible, New International Version®. NIV®. Copyright © 1973, 1978, 1984 by International Bible Society. Used by permission of Zondervan Publishing House. Distributed in the U.K. by permission of Hodder and Stoughton Ltd. All rights reserved. "NIV" is a registered trademark of International Bible Society. UK trademark number 1448790.

This study guide is based on and includes excerpts adapted from The Message of Galatians ©1968 by John R. W. Stott, originally published under the title Only One Way.

Design: Cindy Kiple
Images: Gary S. Chapman/Getty Images

USA ISBN 978-0-8308-2164-8
UK ISBN 978-1-84474-318-6

Printed in the United States of America ∞

P   23   22   21   20   19   18   17   16   15   14   13   12   11   10   9   8   7   6   5   4   3   2

Y   27   26   25   24   23   22   21   20   19   18   17   16   15   14   13   12   11   10   09

Introducing Galatians

Have you ever been led astray? Have you been convinced by a dynamic speaker or a persusasive book only to later find out that it was wrong?

We are most easily convinced when we are young or not well informed on a particular topic. The new Christians in Galatia were in just such a position when false teachers launched an attack on the gospel of grace and the authority of the apostle Paul.

Getting to Know the Galatians
In the course of the thirty years or so which elapsed between his conversion outside Damascus and his imprisonment in Rome, the apostle Paul traveled widely through the empire as an ambassador of Jesus Christ. On his three famous missionary journeys he preached the gospel and planted churches in the provinces of Galatia, Asia, Macedonia (northern Greece) and Achaia (southern Greece). Moreover, his visits were followed by his letters, by which he helped to supervise the churches he founded.

One of these letters, which many believe to be the earliest that he wrote (about A.D. 48 or 49), is the epistle to the Galatians. I believe "Galatia" is a reference to the four citites of Pisidian Antioch, Iconium, Lystra and Derbe, which Paul evangelized during his first missionary journey. You can read about this in Acts 13 and 14.

A Message for Us
The false teaching in Galatia centered on faith versus law. What is required

of us to be Christians? Some were saying we must follow Old Testament law. Again and again Paul directs them back to Jesus Christ as the one who saves.

While the kinds of laws Christians today attempt to follow may differ, this is nonetheless an issue for us. We need to be reminded that we cannot save ourselves through righteous actions. Our only hope of salvation is in Jesus.

Suggestions for Individual Study

1. As you begin each study, pray that God will speak to you through his Word.

2. Read the introduction to the study and respond to the question that follows it. This is designed to help you get into the theme of the study.

3. The studies are written in an inductive format designed to help you discover for yourself what Scripture is saying. Each study deals with a particular passage so that you can really delve into the author's meaning in that context. Read and reread the passage to be studied. The questions are written using the language of the New International Version, so you may wish to use that version of the Bible. The New Revised Standard Version is also recommended.

4. Each study includes three types of questions. *Observation* questions ask about the basic facts: who, what, when, where and how. *Interpretation* questions delve into the meaning of the passage. *Application* questions (also found in the "Apply" section) help you discover the implications of the text for growing in Christ. These three keys unlock the treasures of Scripture.

Write your answers to the study questions in the spaces provided or in a personal journal. Writing can bring clarity and deeper understanding of yourself and of God's Word.

5. In the studies you will find some commentary notes designed to give help with complex verses by giving further biblical and cultural background and contextual information. The notes in the studies are not designed to answer the questions for you. They are to help you along as you learn to study the Bible for yourself. After you have worked through the questions and notes in the guide, you may want to read the accompanying commentary by John Stott in the Bible Speaks Today series. This will give you more information about the text.

6. Move to the "Apply" section. These questions will help you connect the key biblical themes to your own life. Putting the application into practice is one of the keys to growing in Christ.

7. Use the guidelines in the "Pray" section to focus on God, thanking him for what you have learned and praying about the applications that have come to mind.

Suggestions for Members of a Group Study

1. Come to the study prepared. Follow the suggestions for individual study mentioned above. You will find that careful preparation will greatly enrich your time spent in group discussion.

2. Be willing to participate in the discussion. The leader of your group will not be lecturing. Instead, she or he will be encouraging the members of the group to discuss what they have learned. The leader will be asking the questions that are found in this guide.

3. Stick to the topic being discussed. Your answers should be based on the verses which are the focus of the discussion and not on outside authorities such as commentaries or speakers. These studies focus on a particular passage of Scripture. Only rarely should you refer to other portions of the Bible. This allows for everyone to participate on equal ground and for in-depth study.

4. Be sensitive to the other members of the group. Listen attentively when they describe what they have learned. You may be surprised by their insights! Each question assumes a variety of answers. Many questions do not have "right" answers, particularly questions that aim at meaning or application. Instead the questions push us to explore the passage more thoroughly.

When possible, link what you say to the comments of others. Also, be affirming whenever you can. This will encourage some of the more hesitant members of the group to participate.

5. Be careful not to dominate the discussion. We are sometimes so eager to express our thoughts that we leave too little opportunity for others to respond. By all means participate! But allow others to also.

6. Expect God to teach you through the passage being discussed and through the other members of the group. Pray that you will have an enjoyable and profitable time together, but also that as a result of the study you will find ways that you can take action individually and/or as a group.

7. It will be helpful for groups to follow a few basic guidelines. These guidelines, which you may wish to adapt to your situation, should be read at the beginning of the first session.

☐ Anything said in the group is considered confidential and will not be discussed outside the group unless specific permission is given to do so.

☐ We will provide time for each person present to talk if he or she feels comfortable doing so.

☐ We will talk about ourselves and our own situations, avoiding conversation about other people.

☐ We will listen attentively to each other.

☐ We will be very cautious about giving advice.

8. If you are the group leader, you will find additional suggestions at the back of the guide.

1
FALSE TEACHERS & FAITHLESS CHRISTIANS

Galatians 1:1-10

*T*he devil disturbs the church as much by error as by evil. When he cannot entice Christian people into sin, he deceives them with false doctrine.

Reading Galatians 1, you may be surprised to see how the Galatian people have allowed themselves to be turned away from the true gospel by false teachers. Paul's reaction was one of astonishment. Yet this pattern of distorting the gospel continues today. Many evangelists have been similarly distressed to see how quickly, how readily converts relax their hold of the gospel which they seemed to have so firmly embraced. It is, as Paul writes in Galatians 3:1, as if someone has cast a spell over them. By being aware of these dynamics we can keep ourselves from being led astray.

Open
■ How do you "test" the truth of what you hear from public figures, your pastor and other Christian teachers?

Study

■ *Read Galatians 1:1-5.* Since Paul's visit to the Galatian cities, the churches he founded had been troubled by false teachers called Judiazers. The false teachers had launched a powerful attack on Paul's authority and gospel. They contradicted his gospel of justification by grace alone through faith alone, insisting that for salvation more than faith in Christ was needed. You had to be circumcised as well, they said, and keep all the law of Moses. Having undermined Paul's gospel, they proceeded to undermine his authority also. "Who is this fellow Paul, anyway?" they asked scornfully. "He certainly wasn't one of the twelve apostles of Jesus. Nor, so far as we know, has he received any authorization from anybody. He is just a self-appointed imposter."

---

1. What key themes emerge in verses 1-5 in response to the controversy with the false teachers?

---

2. How was it significant in light of the controversy for Paul to say he is an apostle "sent not from men nor by man, but by Jesus Christ and God the Father"?

---

3. Create an outline of the gospel based on verses 1-5.

Summary: What the apostle has in fact done in these introductory verses of the epistle is to trace three stages of divine action of humanity's salvation. Stage 1 is the death of Christ for our sins to rescue us out of this present evil age. Stage 2 is the appointment of Paul as an apostle to bear witness to the Christ who died and rose again. Stage 3 is the gift to us who believe of the grace and peace which Christ won and Paul witnessed to. At each of these three stages the Father and the Son have acted or continue to act together. No wonder Paul ends his first paragraph with a doxology.

---

4. *Read Galatians 1:6-10.* In every other epistle, after greeting his readers, Paul goes on to pray for them or to praise and thank God. In contrast, what does he do in this letter?

---

5. The Greek word in verse 6 for "deserting" means "to transfer one's allegiance." It is used for soldiers in the army who revolt or desert and those who change sides in politics or philosophy. How is it appropriate for the Galatians as they are described here?

---

6. The false teachers were trying to "pervert" the gospel (v. 7) or, according to the Greek, to completely "reverse" the meaning of the gospel. Thus the Galatians were forsaking the gospel of grace for a gospel of works. Fill in this chart, contrasting these two ways of thinking as you understand them.

Grace   **Works**

So the two chief characteristics of the false teachers are that they were troubling the church and changing the gospel. These two go together. You cannot touch the gospel and leave the church untouched, because the church is created and lives by the gospel. Indeed, the church's greatest troublemakers (now as then) are not those outside who oppose, ridicule and persecute it, but those inside who try to change the gospel.

---

7. How do you account for Paul's strong words against the teachers in verses 8-9?

---

8. Verses 8 and 9 tell us that we are to judge the teacher by the gospel and not judge the gospel by them. Why is this distinction important?

---

9. Why does Paul add this "disclaimer" in verse 10?

---

10. The popular view is that there are many ways to God and that the gospel changes with the changing years. How could you argue against that using Paul's perspective in these verses?

Summary: How can we recognize the true gospel? First, it is the gospel of grace, of God's free and unmerited favor. Whenever teachers start exalting humanity, implying that we can contribute anything to our salvation by our own morality, religion, philosophy or respectability, the gospel of grace is being corrupted. Second, the true gospel is the New Testament gospel. The norm by which all systems and opinions are to be tested is the gospel which the apostles preached and which is now recorded in the New Testament. Anyone who rejects the apostolic gospel is to be rejected.

Apply

■ Who do you know who is being swayed by false teaching, and how can you help that person?

When are you likely to judge the gospel according to a teacher rather than judging the teacher by the gospel?

Pray

■ Following Paul's example, list the steps in your life that led you to an understanding of the true gospel. Use this as a source of prayer and praise to God.

2
RADICAL CHANGE

Galatians 1:11-24

So far in his letter to the Galatians, Paul has explained that there is only one gospel, the criterion by which all human opinions are to be tested. Without doubt it is a very wonderful gospel. But where did Paul get it all from? Was it the product of his own fertile brain? Was it stale secondhand stuff with no original authority? Did he steal it from the other apostles in Jerusalem as the false teachers evidently maintained?

To prove that he received his gospel directly from Christ, Paul offers evidence from his own autobiography—his radically changed life.

Open

■ When someone you know undergoes a radical change, what kinds of questions does it raise for you?

Study

■ *Read Galatians 1:11-17.* Paul claims that his gospel, which is being called into question by the Judaizers and deserted by the Galatians, was neither an invention (as if his own brain had fabricated it) nor a tradition (as if the church had handed it down to him), but a revelation (for God had made it known to him). Paul dared to call the gospel he preached "my gospel," not because he had made it up but because it had been uniquely revealed to him.

1. What were the driving forces in Paul's life before his conversion?

2. What evidence is there that God was working in Paul's life even before his conversion to Christ?

3. What steps did Paul take to deliberately avoid human consultation about the gospel?

4. Why does Paul take care in countering the accusations that he got his gospel from someone else?

5. How does Paul's preconversion life add weight to his claim that his gospel came from God?

Summary: Having made the startling claim to a direct revelation from God without human means, Paul goes on to prove it from history, that is, from the facts of his own autobiography. Paul's situation before his conversion, at his conversion and after his conversion show that he clearly got his gospel not from any human being, but direct from God.

6. *Read Galatians 1:18-24.* How does Paul pile up additional evidence that he was not unduly influenced by the apostles or others?

7. At the beginning of his Christian life, Paul did not totally avoid other Christians, but he restricted his contacts. What did his caution accomplish in his life?

8. Paul had a direct revelation from God. How can you use the Scriptures, God's revelation to us, to exercise discernment and wisdom in whom you allow to influence you spiritually?

9. Given his reputation, how might Paul have expected the churches to respond to him as a supposed new believer?

10. What significance do you see in the fact that the Christians in Judea "praised God because of" Paul, rather than praising Paul?

Summary: Before his conversion Saul of Tarsus was a bigot and a fanatic, wholehearted in his devotion to Judaism and in his persecution of Christ and the church. A man in that mental and emotional state is in no mood to change his mind. No conditioned reflex or other psychological device could convert him. Only God could reach him—and God did!

Apply

■ A startling change in a person's life can mean many different things. When has God made a radical change in your life which some people at first didn't understand?

Think of someone you know who has undergone a big change. How can you tell whether that change has been brought about by God or is the result of some human error or sin?

What are the biggest changes which knowing Christ has brought about in your life? Praise God for how he has worked and continues to work in you.

Pray

■ What changes in your life would you still like the Lord to bring about? Pray for your will to be in cooperation with God's workings.

3
ONLY ONE GOSPEL

Galatians 2:1-10

*P*aul's detractors have plenty of successors in the Christian church today. It is fashionable in some quarters to talk about the "Pauline" gospel and the "Petrine" gospel and the "Johannine" gospel, as if they were quite different from one another.

But all this is mistaken.

The apostles of Jesus Christ do not contradict one another in the New Testament. Certainly there are differences in style between them, because their inspiration did not obliterate their individual personality. There are also differences of emphasis, because they were called to different spheres and preached or wrote to different audiences. But they complement one another.

Open

■ What aspects of the gospel sometimes seem contradictory to you, even if intellectually you know they are consistent?

Study

■ One of the ways in which some false teachers of Paul's day tried to undermine his authority was to hint that his gospel was different from Peter's, and indeed from the views of all the other apostles in Jerusalem.

They were trying to disrupt the unity of the apostolic circle.

To prove that his gospel was independent of the other apostles, Paul stressed that he paid only one visit to Jerusalem in fourteen years and that this lasted only fifteen days. To prove that his gospel was yet identical with theirs, he now stresses that when he paid a proper visit to Jerusalem, his gospel was endorsed and approved by them.

1. *Read Galatians 2:1-5.* In this passage, what points is Paul especially striving to get across?

2. Why was it wise for Paul to keep his meeting with the apostles private?

3. What is significant about the apostles' response to Titus?

4. How could Paul have been found to be "running his race in vain"?

5. Paul implies that giving in to the false teachers would mean a descent into slavery. In what senses could a Christian become a slave?

Summary: Paul saw the issue plainly. It was not just a question of circumcision and uncircumcision, of Gentile and Jewish customs. It was a matter of fundamental importance regarding the truth of the gospel, namely, of Christian freedom versus bondage. Acceptance before God depends entirely on God's grace in the death of Jesus Christ received by faith.

Read Galatians 2:6-10. What was the outcome of Paul's consultation with the Jerusalem apostles? Did they contradict Paul's gospel? Did they modify it, edit it, trim it, supplement it? No. Paul says, "Those men added nothing to my message" (v. 6). Further, they gave Paul "the right hand of fellowship" (v. 9). They recognized that they and Paul had been entrusted with the same gospel. The only difference between them was that they had been allocated different spheres in which to preach it.

---

6. What did the apostles in Jerusalem have to be convinced of in order to accept Paul's preaching?

---

7. The approval of Peter, James and John was crucial to the case Paul was making in this letter. Then why does he apparently downplay their importance (v. 6)?

---

8. What distinction do the other apostles see in Paul's ministry (vv. 7-9)?

---

9. What significance do you find in the fact that the apostles accepted Paul's ministry when they saw the grace given to him (v. 9) rather than the persuasive gifts or intelligence or preaching abilities given to him?

---

10. What are some distorted versions of the gospel which you have heard?

11. How did you discover that these versions had altered the true gospel?

12. How would you answer someone who says that the gospel needs to be updated and revised in order to meet changing needs in changing times?

Summary: There is only one gospel, the apostolic faith, a recognizable body of doctrine taught by the apostles of Jesus Christ and preserved for us in the New Testament. If there is only one gospel in the New Testament, there is only one gospel for the church.

Apply —————————————————————————

■ Think of some Christian groups whose style grates on your nerves (for example, their music, preaching, dress, general approach, architecture or worship). How does seeing that there is only one gospel help your acceptance of them?

Think of some Christian groups who choose to emphasize things you don't think are crucial (certain social concerns, doctrinal points, lifestyle issues you consider gray areas). How does seeing that there is only one gospel affect your understanding of them?

Pray —————————————————————————

■ Thank God for your unity with other Christians. Pray that you will increasingly *feel* your unity as well as know about it.

4
FACING CONFLICT

Galatians 2:11-21

W ithout doubt it is one of the most tense and dramatic episodes in the New Testament. Here are Paul and Peter, two leading apostles of Jesus Christ, face to face in complete and open conflict. Both were Christian men, men of God, who knew what it was to be forgiven through Christ and to have received the Holy Spirit. Both were apostles of Jesus Christ, specially called, commissioned and invested with authority by him.

Yet here is the apostle Paul opposing the apostle Peter to his face, contradicting him, rebuking him, condemning him, not because of Peter's teaching, but because of his conduct. There is much for us to learn from this dramatic situation.

Open
■ When have you seen a conflict erupt between church leaders? What was it about, and how was it resolved (if it was)?

Study
1. *Read Galatians 2:11-13.* Describe the situation that concerns Paul.

2. Taking into account Paul's previous meeting with Peter, James and John in Jerusalem (study 3), why would Paul have been especially incensed at Peter's behavior in Antioch?

Only a short while previously, as is recorded in Acts 10 and 11, Peter had been granted a direct, special revelation from God that Gentiles who believed must be welcomed into the Christian church. There is no suggestion in Galatians 2 that Peter had changed his mind. Why then did he withdraw from fellowship with Gentile believers in Antioch?

Paul's charge is that Peter and the others acted in insincerity and not from personal conviction. The Greek word for "insincerity" is the word from which we get the English word *hypocrisy*. Their withdrawal from table-fellowship with Gentile believers was not prompted by any theological principle, but by craven fear of a small pressure group.

---

3. What did Peter have to fear from the circumcision group?

---

4. Why do small pressure groups in the church arouse such fear in the majority and even in the leadership?

---

5. When have you given in to pressure and acted insincerely out of fear, rather than from personal conviction?

Summary: The same Peter who had denied his Lord for fear of a maidservant (Mark 14:66-72) now denied him again for fear of the circumcision group.

He still believed the gospel, but he failed to practice it. If Paul had not taken his stand against Peter that day, either the whole Christian church would have drifted into a Jewish backwater and stagnated, or there would have been a permanent rift between Gentile and Jewish Christendom. Paul's outstanding courage on that occasion in resisting Peter preserved both the truth of the gospel and the international brotherhood and sisterhood of the church.

---

6. *Read Galatians 2:14-16.* What made this issue worth the danger of a public confrontation?

---

7. In some Christian fellowships believers hesitate to confront each other, and in others they confront each other too quickly. What are the spiritual dangers of each approach?

---

8. How would keeping in mind what Paul called "the truth of the gospel" (v. 14) have affected the situations you recalled in questions 4 and 5?

Summary: Paul's opposition to Peter was just the kind of open, head-on collision which the church would seek at any price to avoid today. Paul acted as he did out of a deep concern for the very principle which Peter lacked. Notice the spiritual perception into the fundamental issue—that Peter and the others were not "walking straight" (literally, v. 14) according to the truth of the gospel. Paul is determined to defend and uphold the gospel at all costs, even at the expense of publicly humiliating a brother apostle.

Paul's critics argued like people still argue today: "If God justifies bad people, what is the point of being good? Can't we do as we like and live as we please?" But a person who is united to Christ is never the same person again. It is not just the person's standing before God which has changed; it is the person who has changed—radically, permanently changed. In one sense, we live this new life through faith in Christ. In another sense, it is not we who live it at all, but Christ who lives it in us.

9. *Read Galatians 2:17-21.* Why would the gospel of God's grace bring down the accusation that "Christ promotes sin"?

10. Christians who are sure of their salvation can still be caught sinning. How does Paul deal with that uncomfortable fact?

11. Paul said that he no longer lives, but Christ lives in him (v. 20). How do you reconcile his words with the fact that Paul was still very much alive?

12. Why would Christ have "died for nothing" if righteousness could be gained through keeping the law (v. 21)?

Summary: If God does not require works of the law before he accepts people, how dare we impose a condition on them which he does not impose? If God has accepted them, how can we reject them?

Apply

■ Many are the vocal pressure groups in the contemporary church. We must not be stampeded into submission to them out of fear. If they oppose the truth of the gospel, we must not hesitate to oppose them. When the issue before us is trivial, we must be as pliable as possible. But when the truth of the gospel is at stake, we must stand our ground.

What current pressures are you aware of—on yourself or within your Christian fellowship—to add conditions to the truth of the gospel?

What actions would help to keep accountability in light of those pressures?

Pray

■ In what areas do you need to let Christ more fully live his life through you? Pray that you will live even more deeply "by faith in the Son of God."

5
FAITH & WORKS

Galatians 3:1-14

*D*ear idiots" (J. B. Phillips) begins this section of Galatians. Paul sees the Galatians' turning away from the gospel as an act of spiritual treason (1:6) and folly. Indeed, so stupid was it that Paul wonders if some sorcerer "has bewitched" them. The Galatians knew perfectly well that the gospel is received by faith alone. How could they turn away?

Open
■ In what areas of life are you tempted to try to earn God's favor by your good actions?

Study
■ Throughout most of chapters 1 and 2 Paul has been stoutly defending the divine origin of his apostolic mission and message. Now he comes back to the Galatians and to their unfaithfulness to the gospel as a result of the corrupting influence of the false teachers. Having embraced the truth at the beginning (that sinners are justified by grace, in Christ, through faith), they have now adopted the view that circumcision and the works of the law are also necessary for justification. The essence of Paul's argument is that their new position is a contradiction of the gospel.

1. *Read Galatians 3:1-9.* What words and phrases reveal Paul's attitude toward the Galatians?

2. Twice Paul calls the Galatian Christians "foolish" (vv. 1, 3). In what senses is it foolish to add works to the gospel of Christ?

3. In artwork Christ is portrayed in many ways: teaching crowds, working alongside Joseph in the carpenter shop, praying in Gethsemane, welcoming children, walking on water. Why would Paul choose to focus on portraying Christ as crucified?

The gospel is not good advice to people, but good news about Christ; not an invitation to us to do anything, but a declaration of what God has done; not a demand, but an offer. If the Galatians had grasped the gospel of Christ crucified, that on the cross Christ did everything necessary for our salvation, they would have realized that the only thing required of them was to receive the good news by faith. To add good works to the work of Christ was an offense to his finished work.

4. After beginning our Christian lives by faith, most of us at one time or other imitate the Galatians and fall into relying on our own efforts. Why do you think this happens?

5. To the Judaizers who were misleading the Galatian Christians, Abraham was a hero and patriarch. How does Paul turn the tables and use Abraham as an example of faith instead of lawkeeping?

6. What do we have in common with Abraham?

Summary: All this, the apostle says, the Galatians should have known. They should never have fallen under the spell of these false teachers. Indeed, they would not have done so if they had kept Christ crucified before their eyes. We too should learn to test every theory and teaching by the gospel of Christ crucified, especially as it is known to us from Scripture and from experience.

7. *Read Galatians 3:10-14.* The ugly words *curse* and *cursed* appear often in this passage. What justifies Paul's use of such language?

8. Why is there a curse hanging over those who try to rely on observing the law?

9. The "curse of the law" from which Christ redeemed us must be the curse resting on us for our disobedience (v. 10). And he redeemed us from it by "becoming a curse" himself. He voluntarily took our curse upon himself in order to deliver us from it. What does it mean to you that Christ became a curse for us?

10. What are some differences between law and faith?

11. In your own experience, what does it mean to "live by faith"?

12. What are some obstacles to living by faith?

Summary: No one can be justified before God by works of the law. It is quite true, as an axiom, that "The man who does these things will live by them" (v. 12). But nobody (except Jesus) has ever done them; therefore nobody can live by them. The dreadful function of the law is to condemn, not to justify. Jesus Christ has done for us on the cross what we could not do for ourselves.

Apply —————————————————————————

■ Consider ways that you might have fallen into trying to please God or earn his favor by your own efforts. How does this passage encourage you to examine your heart?

Think of someone you know who is struggling with self-effort. How can you help restore that person to trust in Christ?

Pray —————————————————————————

■ Name all the ways you can think of that Jesus Christ has done for you what you could not do for yourself. Praise him for his sufficiency.

6
THE GIFT
OF THE LAW

Galatians 3:15-29

Some try to go to Jesus without first meeting Moses. They want to skip the Old Testament, to inherit the promise of justification in Christ without the prior pain of condemnation by the law. We need the law to lift off the lid of our respectability and disclose what we are really like underneath—sinful, rebellious, guilty, under the judgment of God and helpless to save ourselves. Not until the law has humbled us even to hell will we turn to the gospel to raise us to heaven.

There are some, however, who go to Moses and the law to be condemned and stay in this unhappy bondage. They are still living in the Old Testament. Their religion is a grievous yoke, hard to be borne. They have never gone to Christ to be set free.

Open
■ Consider the above paragraph describing two responses to God's law. Which one tends to describe your life?

Study
1. *Read Galatians 3:15-22.* Trace the steps of Paul's argument that the

introduction of law through Moses (the "mediator" of v. 19) does not supersede God's promise to Abraham.

The Greek word in verses 15 and 17 is translated "covenant," but it was in common use for a will. (See Hebrews 9:15-17, where the two ideas of a covenant and a will are also linked together.) The point Paul is making is that the wishes and promises which are expressed in a will are unalterable. Paul may be referring to ancient Greek law by which a will, once executed and ratified, could not be revoked or even modified. Or he may be saying that it cannot be altered or annulled by somebody else. God promised an inheritance to Abraham and his posterity. God's purpose was not just to give the land of Canaan to the Jews, but to give salvation (a spiritual inheritance) to believers who are in Christ.

2. Why is a will an appropriate metaphor for the point Paul is making?

3. How is Christ foreshadowed in God's promise to Abraham?

4. God's promise to Abraham was made a very long time ago. How do modern-day Christians still participate in it?

5. Why must we choose between relying on the law and relying on the promise?

6. If God's law can't save anyone, why did God give it to humanity?

Summary: Paul is moving toward the conclusion that the Christian religion is the religion of Abraham and not of Moses, of promise and not of law; and that Christians are enjoying today the promise which God made to Abraham centuries ago. But in this passage, having contrasted these two kinds of religion, he shows the relation between them. After all, the God who gave the promise to Abraham and the God who gave the law to Moses are the same God!

Read Galatians 3:23-29. Paul uses two vivid similes in verses 23 and 24. The law expresses the will of God for his people, telling us what to do and what not to do, and warns us of the penalties of disobedience. But thank God, he never meant this oppression to be permanent. Its purpose was to shut us up in prison until Christ should set us free, or to put us under tutors until Christ should make us God's children.

7. How does law lead us toward Christ?

8. What are some comparisons between being in prison and trying to earn God's favor by following his law?

9. How do people resist the "tutor" which is trying to lead them to Christ?

10. What difference does it make for you to see yourself as a child of God?

11. What difference does it make for you to see other Christians as children of God?

12. Differences of race, social standing and gender obviously exist among Christians. What should be Christians' attitude toward these natural differences?

Summary: Paul has painted a vivid contrast between those who are "under the law" and those who are "in Christ," and everybody belongs to one category or the other. If we are "under the law," our religion is a bondage. But if we are "in Christ," we have been set free. Our religion is characterized by "promise" rather than by "law." We know ourselves related to God and to all God's other children in space, time and eternity.

Apply ───────────────────────────────
■ Not until the law has arrested and imprisoned us will we pine for Christ to set us free. How did God's law lead you to Christ?

In what ways do you find yourself being drawn back under the bondage to law?

Where would you like to see oneness in Christ more of a reality, and what can you do to help it happen?

Pray ────────────────────────────────
■ Praise God for how he faithfully keeps his promises. Pray that you will continually trust his promises.

7
CHILDREN OF GOD
Galatians 4:1-20

*F*ather, I would rather be your slave than your child."

Who among us would make such an odd request of our parents? Yet that was the folly of the Galatians, under the influence of their false teachers.

The way for us to avoid the Galatians' folly is to let God's Word keep telling us what we have and are in Christ. One of the great purposes of daily Bible reading, meditation and prayer is just this, to get ourselves correctly orientated, to remember who and what we are.

Open
■ When and why have you had an especially strong awareness that you are a child of God?

Study
1. *Read Galatians 4:1-11.* What are the key images being used in this passage?

2. Legally, what does it mean to be an heir as a child (minor)?

Even in Old Testament days, before Christ came and when we were under the law, we were heirs—heirs of the promise which God made to Abraham. But we had not yet inherited the promise. We were like children during the years of their minority; our childhood was a form of bondage.

3. What are the differences between the way a slave on an estate and the child of the estate owner would relate to the master (owner)? (Think of differences in conversation together, physical bearing toward each other, attitude toward the estate and how time in each other's presence is spent.)

How does this parallel your relationship with God as his child?

4. What are the "basic principles of the world" (v. 3) which used to hold us in slavery?

5. The term *Abba* (v. 6) is the term Jesus himself used to address God as "Father" when he prayed in Gethsemane (Mark 14:36). How should such intimate terminology affect our prayers?

6. How do you respond to the idea that you not only know God but are known by God (v. 9)? Do you find it comforting? unsettling? cheering?

Summary: The Christian life is the life of sons and daughters; it is not the life of slaves. It is freedom, not bondage. Of course, we are slaves of God, of Christ and of one another. We belong to God, to Christ, to one another, and we love to serve those to whom we belong. But this kind of service is freedom.

7. *Read Galatians 4:12-20.* In what sense(s) did Paul want the Galatians to become like him (v. 12)?

8. What was the contrast between how the Galatians had originally received Paul and how they now regarded him? Why?

9. How could Paul approve of their welcoming him "as if I were an angel of God, as if I were Christ Jesus himself" (v. 14)?

10. What was the contrast between what Paul and his companions wanted for the Galatians and what the false teachers wanted?

11. How does Paul share in the love and suffering of Christ for the Galatians?

12. Why do you think Paul had refused to give up on the Galatian church?

Summary: Paul appeals to the Galatians with immense tenderness. He longed for them to become like him in his Christian faith and life, to be delivered from the evil influence of the false teachers, and to share his convictions about the truth as it is in Jesus, about the liberty with which Christ has made us free. All Christians should be able to say something like this, especially to unbelievers, namely that we are so satisfied with Jesus Christ, with his freedom, joy and salvation, that we want other people to become like us.

Apply

■ In what areas of your life are you enjoying the freedom of a child of God?

In what areas are you still feeling or behaving like a slave, not in the sense of a servant but in the sense of "bondage to the law, as if your salvation hung in the balance"?

What "weak and miserable principles" of your old life has Christ delivered you from?

Pray

■ Pray about your responses above. Ask God to help you in the areas where you face bondage. Let your memories lead you into praise for how he has worked and continues to work in your life.

8
CELEBRATING FREEDOM

Galatians 4:21-31

Many people today *want* to be under the law. They are not, of course, the Jews or Judaizers to whom Paul was writing, but people whose religion is legalistic, who imagine that the way to God is by the observance of certain rules. There are even professing Christians who turn the gospel into law.

In this passage Paul exposes the inconsistency of their position. This is a difficult allegorical passage, but its message is right up to date.

Open
■ List some of the rules and regulations which Christians imagine will make them acceptable to God.

Why do these "laws" have such a persistent appeal?

Study

1. *Read Galatians 4:21-31.* List all the examples of symbolism you note in this passage.

---

2. What are the contrasts between the two women?

---

between the two sons?

---

3. How does Paul use the history of Abraham's two sons, Ishmael and Isaac, to illustrate the supremacy of promise over law? (See Genesis 15—17 and 21:1-21 for background.)

---

4. How does Paul demonstrate that physical descent from Abraham is not enough to make someone a child of God?

---

5. Note verse 29. The son born "in the ordinary way," Ishmael, would have been seventeen, and Isaac would have been three. What was the conflict between the two sons?

6. Why does conflict persist between followers of the old and new covenants?

An understanding of the Bible is impossible without an understanding of the two covenants. After all, our Bibles are divided in half, into the Old and New Testaments, meaning the Old and New "Covenants." A covenant is a solemn agreement between God and human beings by which he makes them his people and promises to be their God. God established the old covenant through Moses and the new covenant through Christ, whose blood ratified it. The old (Mosaic) covenant was based on law; in it God laid the responsibility on people and said, "Thou shalt . . . , thou shalt not . . ." But the new (Christian) covenant is based on promise; in the promise God keeps the responsibility himself and says, "I will . . . , I will . . . "

7. What is the destiny of those "born in the ordinary way" (not born spiritually in Christ)?

8. What are some ways that religious legalists persecute those who have found freedom in Christ?

In this passage there are not only two covenants mentioned, but two Jerusalems also. Jerusalem, of course, was the capital city which God chose for the land that he gave to his people. It was natural that the word *Jerusalem* should stand for God's people, just as *Moscow* stands for the Russian people or *Washington* for the people of the United States. But who are the people of God? God's people under the old covenant were the Jews, but his people under the new covenant are Christians, believers. Both are "Jerusalem," but the old covenant people of God, the Jews, are "the present Jerusalem," the earthly city, whereas the new covenant people of God, the Christian church, are "the Jerusalem above," the heavenly. Thus the two women, Hagar and Sarah, the mothers of Abraham's two sons, stand for the two covenants, the old and the new, and the two Jerusalems, the earthly and the heavenly.

---

9. What will be the outcome for those who believe God's promises rather than depending on law?

---

10. In what ways have you seen, or even experienced firsthand, conflict and misunderstanding between legalistic Christians and those who know God's grace and are trusting his promises? How was it handled, and with what outcome?

Summary: The persecution of the true church, of Christian believers who trace their spiritual descent from Abraham, is not always by the world, who are strangers unrelated to us, but by our half-siblings, religious people, the nominal church. The religion of Ishmael is a religion of nature, of what human beings can do by themselves without any special intervention of God. But the religion of Isaac is a religion of grace, of what God has done and does, a religion of divine initiative and divine intervention, for Isaac was born supernaturally through a divine promise. And this is what Christianity is, not natural religion but supernatural. Everyone is either an Ishmael or an Isaac, either still what they are by nature or set free by the grace of God. We must seek to be like Isaac, not like Ishmael. We must put our trust in God through Jesus Christ. Only in Christ can we inherit the promises, receive the grace and enjoy the freedom of God.

Apply
■ How do you usually respond to legalism?

How can "free" Christians guard against their own kind of self-righteousness, feeling superior to legalists?

Pray
■ As you praise God for your freedom in Christ, ask him for wisdom to see any pitfalls. Pray for his protection in your spirit and in your relationships.

9
TRUE & FALSE RELIGION

Galatians 5:1-15

*T*he false teachers in the Galatian churches, as we have already seen, were saying that Christian converts had to be circumcised. You might think this is a very trivial matter. Why did Paul make so much fuss and bother about it? Because of its doctrinal implications. As the false teachers were pressing it, circumcision was neither a physical operation, nor a ceremonial rite, but a theological symbol. It stood for a particular type of religion, namely salvation by good works in obedience to the law.

Paul answered that you cannot add circumcision (or anything else, for that matter) to Christ as necessary to salvation, because Christ is sufficient for salvation in himself. If you add anything to Christ, you lose Christ. Salvation is in Christ alone by grace alone through faith alone.

Open

■ Different branches of the Christian church practice various ceremonies and observe various scruples according to conscience. How do you discern whether a custom or practice has become elevated to something necessary for salvation?

Study

1. *Read Galatians 5:1-6.* What is Paul expressing concern about in these verses?

2. The freedom described in verse 1 is not primarily a freedom from sin, but rather from the law. What Christ has done in liberating us is not so much to set our *will* free from the bondage of sin as to set our *conscience* free from the guilt of sin. What words and phrases throughout this passage indicate what it means to be free?

3. Most people value their freedom very highly. Why would anyone need to be warned to stand fast and avoid submitting to slavery?

4. How could Jesus Christ ever be said to be "of no value" (v. 2)?

5. How do you interpret Paul's phrase "fallen away from grace" (v. 4)?

6. How does Paul's tone change in verses 5 and 6?

7. If we have been declared righteous in Christ, why would Paul say that we still hope for it (v. 5)?

Summary: When a person is in Christ, nothing more is necessary. Neither circumcision nor uncircumcision can improve our standing before God. We wait for our future salvation, the hope of spending eternity with Christ in heaven. We do not work for it; we wait for it by faith.

8. *Read Galatians 5:7-12.* In this section the contrast is between "the one who is throwing you into confusion" (the false teacher) and Paul himself, who is teaching the truth of God. How does the race image highlight the problem?

9. How could Paul be so sure that the "persuasion" of the false teachers was not from God, who had called the Galatians?

10. What is the significance of the "yeast" in the "dough" (v. 9)?

11. What was Paul falsely being accused of, and how does he respond (vv. 11-12)?

Summary: Paul is quite sure that error is not going to triumph but that the Galatians will come to a better mind and that the false teacher, however exalted his rank, will fall under the judgment of God. Meanwhile Paul was being persecuted. People hate to be told that they can be saved only at the foot of the cross, and they oppose the preacher who tells them so. The good news of Christ crucified is still an offense to human pride. If we preach this gospel, we shall arouse ridicule and opposition. Christianity will not allow us to sit on the fence or live in a haze; it urges us to be definite and decisive, to choose between a religion of human achievement and a religion of divine achievement.

Read Galatians 5:13-15. What sort of freedom is Christian freedom? Primarily it is a freedom of conscience. What Christ has done in liberating us is not so much to set our will free from the bondage of sin as to set our conscience free from the guilt of sin.

---

12. What are some ways in which the misuse of Christian freedom could lead to self-indulgence?

---

13. How could freedom degenerate to Christians attacking one another (v. 15)?

---

14. Why is "love your neighbor as yourself" an appropriate summary of God's law?

Summary: Every single Christian brother and sister has been called by God and called to freedom. It is freedom from the awful bondage of having to merit the favor of God; it is not freedom from all controls. It is a remarkable paradox. For from one point of view Christian freedom is a form of slavery—not slavery to our sinful nature, but to our neighbor. We are free in relation to God but slaves in relation to each other.

Apply

■ What are your greatest hopes in Christ?

The Judaizers were trying to make circumcision a requirement for salvation. Where are you in the greatest danger of imposing a requirement like the Judaizers? (Consider both positives and negatives—behaviors which Christians "must" do and "must not" do.)

Where are you inclined to indulge yourself in the name of your freedom in Christ?

Who can you serve this week in the freedom of Christian love?

Pray

■ Pray for vigilance against misusing your freedom in Christ. Ask God to keep you alert for self-indulgence and for the tendency to condemn others for their freedom.

10
THE FLESH
& THE SPIRIT

Galatians 5:16-25

*I*nternal war. Some teachers maintain that the Christian has no conflict within because (they say) the flesh has been defeated and the old nature is dead. The passage in this study contradicts such a view.

According to Luther, Christian people are not "stocks and stones," that is, people who "are never moved with anything, never feel any lust or desires of the flesh" (*Commentary on the Epistle to the Galatians*). The flesh and the Spirit remain, and the conflict between them is fierce and unremitting. Yet as we learn to walk in the Spirit, the flesh becomes increasingly subdued.

Open
■ For some Christians the Holy Spirit is the vaguest member of the Trinity. For others he is vital to their experience in Christ. How do you see the Holy Spirit in his involvement with your spiritual life?

Study

■ Each time Paul writes of liberty he adds a warning that it can very easily be lost. Some relapse from liberty into bondage (5:1); others turn their liberty into license (5:13). True Christian liberty expresses itself in self-control, loving service of our neighbor and obedience to the law of God. The question now is: how are these things possible? And the answer is: by the Holy Spirit. He alone can keep us truly free.

Read Galatians 5:16-18. The combatants in the Christian conflict are "the sinful nature" (in some translations "the flesh")—what we are by nature and inheritance, our fallen condition—and "the Spirit"—the Holy Spirit, who renews and regenerates us, first giving us a new nature and then remaining to dwell in us. These two, the flesh and the Spirit, are in sharp opposition to each other.

---

1. What are the causes of the Christian's inner moral conflict?

---

2. What are some practical results of the conflict?

---

3. All Christians have the unhappy experience of discovering that we want God's will but have failed to do it. When we get that insight into ourselves, what are some typical ways we respond?

---

4. According to this passage, how should we respond to such an insight?

5. How do you interpret the difference between living by the Spirit (v. 16) and being led by the Spirit (v. 18)?

6. What hope does the promise of verse 16 offer a believer?

Summary: The conflict between the Spirit and the sinful nature is a specifically Christian conflict. There is such a thing as moral conflict in non-Christian people, but it is fiercer in Christians because they possess two natures—flesh and Spirit—in irreconcilable antagonism.

7. *Read Galatians 5:19-25.* What is the root of the contrast between the two ways of living described here?

The acts of the sinful nature are obvious to all. While our old nature itself is secret and invisible, its works, the words and deeds in which it erupts, are public and evident. The sins Paul lists are in the four realms of sex, religion, society and drink. By contrast, Paul gives a cluster of nine Christian graces which seem to portray a Christian's attitude to God, to other people and to self.

8. Consider the areas of sex, religion, society and drink. Why is each especially vulnerable to corruption by the sinful nature?

9. In Paul's warning "those who live like this" (v. 21), the Greek verb refers to habitual practice rather than an isolated lapse. Why is the distinction important?

10. Consider the character qualities which are called "the fruit of the Spirit" in verses 22 and 23. What is significant about the fact that they are called "fruit" (in contrast with the "acts" of the sinful nature)?

11. Why is crucifixion (v. 24) an apt description of what must happen to the sinful nature?

12. How do the fruit of the Spirit counteract the destructive effects of the acts of the sinful nature?

13. How do the fruit of the Spirit make us Christlike in our attitude toward God?

toward other people?

toward ourselves?

Summary: If we were left to ourselves, we could not do what we would; instead, we would succumb to the desires of our old nature. But if we "live by the Spirit," then we shall not gratify the desires of the sinful nature. We shall still experience them, but we shall not indulge them. On the contrary, we shall bear the fruit of the Spirit.

Apply
■ Which of the acts of the sinful nature are you particularly susceptible to?

Which of the fruit of the Spirit have you sensed in yourself or been told that others see in you?

Which of the fruit of the Spirit do you chronically lack?

How will you choose to live by the Spirit today and the rest of this week?

Pray
■ Thank God for his constant grace in Christ, which covers your failures. Thank him also for his protection, which has kept you from many spiritual dangers.

11
LOVING ONE ANOTHER

Galatians 5:26—6:5

*T*he first and great evidence of our walking by the Spirit or being filled with the Spirit is not some private mystical experience of our own, but our practical relationships of love with other people. Since the first fruit of the Spirit is love, this is only logical. But it is easy to talk about "love" in an abstract and general way; it is much harder to get down to concrete, particular situations in which we actually demonstrate our love for one another. It is some of these which Paul now unfolds.

Open
■ How has the Holy Spirit helped you love someone you would otherwise not find very lovable?

Study
1. *Read Galatians 5:26—6:5.* In this passage, what positive and negative commands does Paul give the Galatians?

2. Why would conceit lead us to provoke and envy each other (5:26)?

___

3. How would you describe a person who is spiritual in a Christian sense (6:1)?

___

4. What temptations accompany seeing another Christian's sin (6:1)?

___

5. Catching someone in sin would require confrontation, perhaps strong words such as Paul had with Peter (Galatians 2:11). How can gentleness enter into restoration?

___

6. What does Paul suggest as a cure for pride over another person's falling into sin (6:3)?

___

Some people think it a sign of fortitude not to bother other people with their burdens. This is more stoical than Christian. It is also true that we should cast all our burdens on Jesus Christ, since he cares for us. But one of the ways in which Jesus bears these burdens of ours is through human friendship.

___

7. When is it hard for you to ask others for help (6:2)?

8. How can Paul say a Christian is "nothing" (6:3)?

9. What are some practical steps we can take to test our own actions (6:4)?

10. Pride is not usually considered a Christian characteristic. What sort of pride is Paul talking about in verse 4?

11. What dangers are inherent in comparing ourselves with others (6:4)?

12. Verse 2 tells us to carry each other's burdens, while verse 5 says we have to carry our own loads. The Greek word in verse 2 means a weight or heavy load, while the Greek word in verse 5 is a common term for a person's pack. So there is no contradiction. We are to bear one another's burdens, which are too heavy for each of us to bear alone; but we cannot share the burden of our own responsibility to God. What are some examples of burdens which Christians can and should carry for each other?

What sorts of burdens should not be shared?

13. Reconsider the fruit of the Spirit from study 10 (Galatians 5:22-23). In this passage, which of them is Paul calling on the Galatians to exercise?

Summary: Truly Christian relationships are governed not by rivalry but by service. The correct attitude is not "I'm better than you and I'll prove it," but "You are a person of importance in your own right (because God made you in his own image and Christ died for you), and it is my joy and privilege to serve you." If we walked by the Spirit, we would love one another more, and if we loved one another more, we would bear one another's burdens, and if we bore one another's burdens, we would not shrink from seeking to restore a Christian who has fallen into sin. By such practical Christian living, the law of Christ is fulfilled.

Apply ——————————————————————————

■ To love one another as Christ loved us may lead us not to some heroic, spectacular deed of self-sacrifice, but to the much more mundane and unspectacular ministry of burden-bearing. When we see somebody with a heavy burden on the heart or mind, we must be ready to get alongside that person and share the burden. Similarly, we must be humble enough to let others share ours.

What burdens of your own do you need to share with others?

Whose burdens can you help carry today?

Pray ——————————————————————————

■ Who do you know who needs to be restored in the sense Paul used here? Pray for that person and what part God might want you to have in restoring them.

Think of someone you tend to provoke and someone you tend to envy. How might conceit be involved in your responses to those people? Pray for understanding into your own heart.

12
SOWING & REAPING

Galatians 6:6-18

We reap what we sow. If we are faithful and conscientious in our sowing, then we can confidently expect a good harvest. If we "sow wild oats," as we sometimes say, then we must not expect to reap strawberries! On the contrary, "those who plough evil and those who sow trouble reap it" (Job 4:8).

In this final section of Galatians Paul has a few final admonitions. At first sight, these instructions and exhortations appear to be very loosely connected, even totally disconnected. But the connecting link is the great principle of sowing and reaping, the principle of order and consistency which is written into all life, material and moral.

Open ───────────────────────────

■ When have you seen "good sowing" produce "good reaping"?

Study ───────────────────────────

■ *Read Galatians 6:6-10.* If farmers want a bumper harvest of a particular grain, then they must sow not only the right seed, but good seed and that plentifully. Only if they do this can they expect a good crop. Precisely the same principle operates in the moral and spiritual sphere. It is not the reapers who decide what the harvest is going to be like, but the sowers.

1. What various contrasts does Paul draw in this passage?

2. How does verse 6 apply to people in the Christian ministry and those who benefit from their ministry?

3. What are some ways that people imagine they can mock God (v. 7)?

4. Verse 8 is obviously not talking about literal seed. Then what sorts of things are "sown"?

5. What are some examples of both bad and good reaping (v. 8)?

6. What are some ways that we can get tired from doing good (v. 9)?

7. Why should "the family of believers" deserve our special attention (v. 10)?

Summary: We are not the helpless victims of our nature, temperament and environment. On the contrary, what we become depends largely on how we behave; our character is shaped by our conduct. How can we expect to reap the fruit of the Spirit if we do not sow in the field of the Spirit? Holiness is a harvest; whether we reap it or not depends almost entirely on what and where we sow.

Read Galatians 6:11-18. Now Paul takes the pen from his secretary's hand in order to add a personal postscript. His "large letters" may actually refer to his handwriting, or the phrase may mean that Paul wants to especially emphasize what he is going to say next. The vital issues at stake are two questions: Is the essence of the Christian religion outward or inward? And is it human or divine—fundamentally a matter of what we do for God or of what he has done for us?

---

8. How did Paul appraise the motives of the Judaizers who insisted on circumcision (vv. 12-13)?

---

9. How would outward keeping of the law avoid persecution for the cross (v. 12)?

---

10. How could Paul "boast" in the cross of Christ (v. 14)?

---

11. What are some examples of "outward" religion which people mistake for true Christianity?

12. How can the church experience peace and mercy (v. 16)?

Summary: It is natural to fallen humanity to decline from the real, the inward and the spiritual, and to fabricate a substitute religion which is easy and comfortable because its demands are external and ceremonial only. But outward things matter little in comparison with the new creation or the new birth.

Apply ————————————————————————

■ In your own experience, what outward signs or works are you tempted to substitute for inner spiritual reality?

Consider accomplishments you are tempted to boast about. How can you turn those around and give credit to Christ?

Pray ————————————————————————

■ Praise God for making you a new creation in Jesus Christ. Pray that your life in Christ will take precedence over everything else.

Guidelines for Leaders

My grace is sufficient for you. (2 Corinthians 12:9)

If leading a small group is something new for you, don't worry. These sessions are designed to be led easily. Because the Bible study questions flow from observation to interpretation to application, you may feel as if the studies lead themselves.

You don't need to be an expert on the Bible or a trained teacher to lead a small group discussion. As a leader, you can guide group members to discover for themselves what the Bible has to say and to listen for God's guidance. This method of learning will allow group members to remember much more of what is said than a lecture would.

This study guide is flexible. You can use it with a variety of groups—students, professionals, neighborhood or church groups. Each study takes forty-five to sixty minutes in a group setting.

There are some important facts to know about group dynamics and encouraging discussion. The suggestions listed below should equip you to effectively and enjoyably fulfill your role as leader.

Preparing for the Study

1. Ask God to help you understand and apply the passage in your own life. Unless this happens, you will not be prepared to lead others. Pray too for the various members of the group. Ask God to open your hearts to the message of his Word and motivate you to action.

2. Read the introduction to the entire guide to get an overview of the topics that will be explored.

3. As you begin each study, read and reread the assigned Bible passage to familiarize yourself with it.

4. This study guide is based on the New International Version of the Bible. It will help you and the group if you use this translation as the basis for your study and discussion.

5. Carefully work through each question in the study. Spend time in meditation and reflection as you consider how to respond.

6. Write your thoughts and responses in the space provided in the study guide. This will help you to express your understanding of the passage clearly.

7. You may want to get a copy of the Bible Speaks Today commentary by John Stott that supplements the Bible book you are studying. The commentary is divided into short units on each section of Scripture so you can easily read the appropriate material each week. This will help you answer tough questions about the passage and its context.

It may help to have a Bible dictionary handy. Use it to look up any unfamiliar words, names or places. (For additional help on how to study a passage, see *How to Lead a LifeGuide Bible Study* from InterVarsity Press, USA.)

8. Take the "Apply" portion of each study seriously. Consider how you need to apply the Scripture to your life. Remember that the group members will follow your lead in responding to the studies. They will not go any deeper than you do.

Leading the Study

1. Begin the study on time. Open with prayer, asking God to help the group to understand and apply the passage.

2. Be sure that everyone in your group has a study guide. Encourage the group to prepare beforehand for each discussion by reading the introduction to the guide and by working through the questions in each study.

3. At the beginning of your first time together, explain that these studies are meant to be discussions, not lectures. Encourage the members of the group to participate. However, do not put pressure on those who may be hesitant to speak during the first few sessions.

4. Have a group member read aloud the introduction at the beginning of the discussion.

5. Every session begins with an "open" question, which is meant to be asked before the passage is read. These questions are designed to introduce the theme of the study and encourage group members to begin to open up. Encourage as many members as possible to participate, and be ready to get the discussion going with your own response.

These opening questions can reveal where our thoughts or feelings need to be transformed by Scripture. That is why it is especially important not to read the passage before the question is asked. The passage will tend to color the honest reactions people would otherwise give because they are, of course, supposed to think the way the Bible does.

6. Have a group member read aloud the passage to be studied.

7. As you ask the study questions, keep in mind that they are designed to be used just as they are written. You may simply read them aloud. Or you may prefer to express them in your own words.

There may be times when it is appropriate to deviate from the study guide. For example, a question may have already been answered. If so, move on to the next question. Or someone may raise an important question not covered in the guide. Take time to discuss it, but try to keep the group from going off on tangents.

8. Avoid answering your own questions. If necessary repeat or rephrase them until they are clearly understood. Or point the group to the commentary woven into the guide to clarify the context or meaning without answering the question. An eager group quickly becomes passive and silent if members think the leader will do most of the talking.

9. Don't be afraid of silence in response to the discussion questions. People may need time to think about the question before formulating their answers.

10. Don't be content with just one answer. Ask, "What do the rest of you think?" or "Anything else?" until several people have given answers to the question.

11. Acknowledge all contributions. Try to be affirming whenever possible. Never reject an answer. If it is clearly off-base, ask, "Which verse led you to that conclusion?" or again, "What do the rest of you think?"

12. Don't expect every answer to be addressed to you, even though this will probably happen at first. As group members become more at ease, they will begin to truly interact with each other. This is one sign of healthy discussion.

13. Don't be afraid of controversy. It can be very stimulating. If you don't resolve an issue completely, don't be frustrated. Explain that the group will move on and God may enlighten all of you in later sessions.

14. Periodically summarize what the group has said about the passage. This helps to draw together the various ideas mentioned and gives continuity to the study. But don't preach.

15. Conclude your time together with conversational prayer, adapting the prayer suggestion at the end of the study to your group. Ask for God's help in following through on the commitments you've made.

16. End on time.

Many more suggestions and helps can be found in *How to Lead a LifeGuide Bible Study* and *The Big Book on Small Groups* (both from InterVarsity Press, USA) or *Housegroups* (Crossway Books, UK). Reading through one of these books would be worth your time.